Mid September 2023 we noticed increased activity around our verandah. After many attempts, one morning we noticed that the willy wagtails had cracked it, the nest had begun!

The birds worked together, taking it in turns.

Gathering materials and carefully sculpting the nest inside and out.

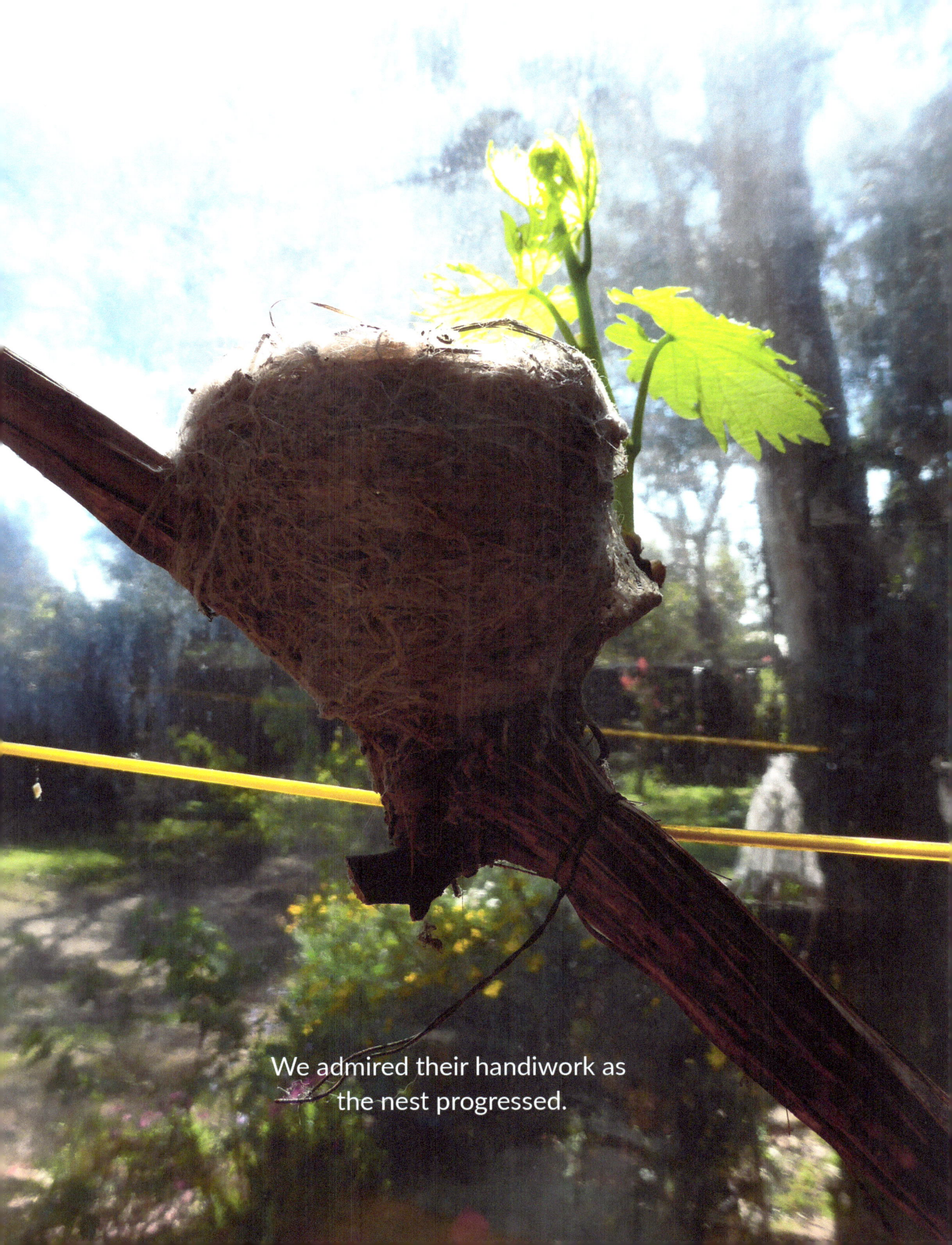

We admired their handiwork as the nest progressed.

They used spider web, feathers, bits of bark stripped from the grapevine and even some of Sparky, the King Charles spaniel's, fur!

Then the sitting began - changing overy every 15 minutes the birds were attentive and protective for the next 7 days.

28/9/23

29/9/23

1/10/23

On 13 October I noticed a lot of activity - there was excitement in the air - something had changed...

...lo and behold, 2 eggs had hatched! They were very ugly chicks - the parents were now busy in a different way, the chicks had to be fed and the new brood protected.

13 October

14 October

15 October

Airconditioning!

And the nest quickly filled

16 October

17 October

18 October

A kookaburra stoically ignored the relentless divebombing and noise Dad was making!

Feeding was constant and
our verandah a rich source
of food!

18 October - the chicks starting to peak over the top of the nest...

19 October

20 October

21 October

One morning it was very windy in the garden. I noticed a great drama taking place...willy wagtails vs ravens vs possum! Who would win?

At one point the possum even fell out of the tree! Pursued by two ravens it scuttled back up the tree trunk to relative safety.

A final standoff before victory to the willy wagtails. At this point I think the possum was thinking 'phew'! 'The enemy of my enemy is my friend!'

21 October

22 October

23 October

Sue arrived one day with live crickets and meal worms. I couldn't believe that the willy wagtails would catch them but they did!

As quickly as we put one on the table, the bird was down, grabbed it and back to feed the voracious babies! The next evening when I sat outside the bird came to the table asking for more! So special to be part of this encounter.

Housekeeping fun fact:

Ever wondered how the nest doesn't fill up with baby bird poo? After being fed the baby bird lifts it's tail, the parent grabs the poo in it's beak, flies off and drops it nearby before returning to the nest - such a neat and efficient operation!

Butterflies were a
favourite food,
watching the chase
was impressive!

24 October

25 October

26 October

Magpie larks with their babies and a pair of lorikeets joined the birdlife in the garden. One cheeky lorikeet came to the dining room window wanting attention! Clearly they posed no threat to the willy wagtails, unlike ravens and kookaburras!

27 October - I went to take my daily photo and saw the first baby fl
Couldn't catch that on camera!!

With the baby birds fledging the parents were even more aggressive and attentive.

Richard had to take protection when he went to the compost bin!! The first baby quickly found a nearby tree. The second flew to the ground causing the parents some consternation before flying up into an old bird cage!

Don't mess with me or my babies!

By lunchtime one baby bird was left in the nest.

It sat on the side for quite awhile, seemingly very comfortable and reluctant to leave!

The baby tested it's wings...and was given a demo on what to do. It practised standing on the side of the nest.
Even with encouragement it seemed in no hurry to fly...and why would it? Food was still being delivered!
Meanwhile, the adults continued feeding the other two young ones in the nearby trees.

26 October - the baby ventured onto a nearby branch...

...getting a little braver as the day progressed.

The cage was a great spot to land on a maiden flight!

Two babies waiting for their sibling

Siblings reunited - a lot more room to move now!

Watching on as a new phase begins!

At first the babies were tentative and stayed together in the nearby trees with their parents ever watchful.

As they got braver they ventured onto the fence.

This became one of their favouritr meal spots!

The old bird cage was another great place to hang out - perhaps this had something to do with the great food delivery service!

Life was busy for the family.

Watching out for food

Warning off threats!

Bug catching lessons

Flying lessons

During the two weeks after they fledged, we watched the chicks growing daily as they learnt more and more. Gradually they even started to sound like grown up birds!

They ventured further into the garden

There was a lot of sitting around!

There was
always plenty
of action in
the pursuit of
bugs!

And more sitting around...before finally heading off...after all that activity, the garden seemed strangely quiet!

On 6 December we noticed a lot of activity in the verandah once again - a new pair were renovating the nest!

12 December - 2 eggs had been laid with the first baby hatching on Christmas Eve and the second on Christmas Day.

We had our family Christmas lunch outside as we watched the willy wagtails feed their newborns!

On New Years Day we noticed that there was only one adult coming and going. The single mother was now raising the new chicks - we didn't want to think too much about what might have happened to the other adult bird!

As the babies grew, feeding was even more constant! The mother bird was adept at catching dragon flies - try feeding one of those to a baby - they have wings that stick out sideways!
One of the lorikeets came to see how things were going

Dragonfly breakfast!

Thinking about flying...

7 January 2024. A lot of wing testing and once again baby birds are ready to fly.
8 January - tentative flights along the vine and then they were off!
This time the babies didn't hang around the garden.
Well done Mum!

Once again the nest is empty, we wonder if it will be
occupied again next year!!

2022

Watching these birds at such close quarters was such a joy. in 2022 they had tried to build a nest in a couple of places in the verandah and had not succeeded - but they did bring their babies to the neary trees and we watched them being fed and learning to fly across our spa fence.

www.ingramcontent.com/pod-product-compliance
Lightning Source LLC
Chambersburg PA
CBHW041543260326

41914CB00015B/1537